The Impact of a Life

A Memorial Journal

REGINA C. CASTRO

WestBow Press books may be ordered through booksellers or by contacting:

WestBow Press
A Division of Thomas Nelson & Zondervan
1663 Liberty Drive
Bloomington, IN 47403
www.westbowpress.com
844-714-3454

Interior Image Credit: Donald Franklin Lane 1968-2016

NIV:
• Scripture quotations taken from The Holy Bible, New International Version® NIV® Copyright © 1973 1978 1984 2011 by Biblica, Inc. TM. Used by permission. All rights reserved worldwide.

ISBN: 978-1-6642-3936-4 (sc)
ISBN: 978-1-6642-3938-8 (hc)
ISBN: 978-1-6642-3937-1 (e)

Library of Congress Control Number: 2021913483

Print information available on the last page.

WestBow Press rev. date: 08/16/2021

WESTBOW
PRESS®
A DIVISION OF THOMAS NELSON
& ZONDERVAN

Do not be anxious about anything, but in every situation, by prayer and petition, with thanksgiving, present your requests to God.

And the peace of God, which transcends all understanding, will guard your hearts and your minds in Christ Jesus.

Finally, brothers and sisters, whatever is true, whatever is noble, whatever is right, whatever is pure, whatever is lovely, whatever is admirable—if anything is excellent or praiseworthy—think about such things. (Philippians 4:6–8 NIV)

Contents

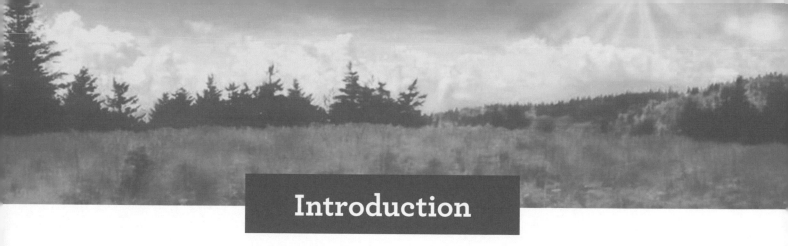

Introduction

I was awakened early one morning while dreaming of my late grandfather. My papaw was an incredibly kind and patient man. I have so many fond memories of him. In my dream, I was at my mamaw's house after his passing, and many relatives and friends were milling about the home. As people told stories about my papaw, I told everyone to wait just a minute. I ran to grab a notebook and pen, then I began writing down their wonderful, treasured memories.

After I awoke, I thought what a great idea it would be to have a way to document our loved ones' lives and the stories, sayings, and lessons that they shared while they were here. It would be such a treasure to help those left behind remember how wonderful their loved ones' lives had been. This is especially important because storytelling is part of the process of healing.

I hope you and your family find healing and share a few smiles while sharing the memories that made your loved one the special person they were.

How to Use This Journal

This journal is a simple way to record the memories that you do not want to forget. As time goes by, our memories tend to fade. This book will allow you and those who knew your loved one to jot down all those valuable stories. When you open the book, the first thing you will do is write a short biography telling of the most important highlights of their life. After that, you will find a place to affix the obituary and a favorite picture. On the following pages, there are places to record their favorite sayings and the lessons they taught those around them. The blank memory pages are a more informal place for friends and family to jot down treasured moments with many different people. This book of memories will provide you with a snapshot of the special life of your loved one.

In Loving Memory of

_____

Born: _____

Passed Away: _____

The Story of _____

Write a short biography of your loved one's life. Include important details such as when and where they were born, married, or when any other pivotal moments in their life occurred.

_____
_____
_____
_____
_____
_____
_____
_____
_____
_____
_____
_____
_____
_____
_____
_____
_____
_____
_____

Insert
Obituary
Here

Insert
Photo
Here

FAMILY TREE

_____

Mother: _____   Father: _____

Grandmother: _____   Grandmother: _____

Grandfather: _____   Grandfather: _____

Grandmother's Mother: Grandmother's Mother:

_____   _____

Grandmother's Father: Grandmother's Father:

_____   _____

Grandfather's Mother: Grandfather's Mother:

_____   _____

Grandfather's Father: Grandfather's Father:

_____   _____

G- Grandmother's Mother: G-Grandmother's Mother:

_____   _____

G-Grandmother's Father: G-Grandmother's Father:

_____   _____

G-Grandfather's Mother: G-Grandfather's Mother:

_____   _____

G-Grandfather's Father: G-Grandfather's Father:

_____   _____

Sayings

Use this page to record the common phrases or sayings that your loved one used.

_____
_____
_____
_____
_____
_____
_____
_____
_____
_____
_____
_____
_____
_____
_____
_____
_____
_____
_____
_____
_____
_____
_____
_____
_____
_____
_____
_____
_____
_____
_____

Lessons They Taught

Use this page to record the important lessons that they taught.

Memories of Friends and Family

On these pages, please have your friends and family freely write any memories that they have. Feel free to pass this book around to get everyone's experiences written down.

Memories

Memories

Memories

Memories

Memories

They Were From ...

Use this easy-to-follow template to create a unique poem about your loved one. These poems are inspired by the poem "Where I'm From" by George Ella Lyon.

They were from _____
list several important items from their childhood.

They were from _____
list things that could be found around their childhood home.

They were from _____
list things found outside their childhood home.

They were from _____
list important events for the family.

They were from _____
list people who were important to your loved one.

They were from _____
list sayings or inside jokes of the family.

They were from _____
list favorite family foods.

They were from _____
create an ending that showcases the things that were most important to the family.

The Neighborhood

Add pictures, maps, or newspaper clippings of the childhood home and neighborhood.

Treasured Photos and Mementos

Treasured Photos and Mementos

Treasured Photos and Mementos

Treasured Photos and Mementos

About the Author

I am from rhododendrons, old quilts, dulcimers, and cool night air.

I am from rockin' chairs, front porch swings, cannin' jars, and breakin' beans.

I am from tobacco barns, Sunday dinner after church, and the moan of the slow freight train.

I am from Papaws and Mamaws and Mama and Daddy, a sister to some and a friend to many.

I am from "Upon my honor," "Mark my words," and "Do you want a spankin'?"

I am from "Go get me a switch" and armpit pinches during church.

I am from banana puddin', fried green tomatoes, and chicken 'n' dumplins.

I am from countless pictures in an old cedar chest of weddings, deaths, reunions at the church, baptisms in the river, and the knowledge that we will *all* be together again.

Printed in the United States
by Baker & Taylor Publisher Services